Imagine a Garden

Contents

Written by Poppy O'Neill

Illustrated by Linh Nguyen

Collins

1 What is meditation?

Meditation is a technique for focusing your **attention** and clearing your mind. When you meditate, you relax your mind and body, and any thoughts and feelings you're experiencing become quieter. Focusing your attention on one thing – like a sound or an image – can help to quiet your thoughts and feelings. Rest and reflection time allows us to pause from our busy lives and to be more present in the here and now.

There are lots of different ways to meditate.

Sitting meditation: usually done with your eyes closed

Walking meditation: involves focusing on each step you take

Guided meditation: another person talks you through the meditation

Body scan meditation: focuses on the sensations in your body

Visualisation: involves using your imagination to picture somewhere calm

You'll find a bit of all of these kinds of meditation in this book.

2 Where does meditation come from?

The earliest records of people meditating are from what is now India and Pakistan, and date back as far as 5000 BCE. Wall art has been found showing people sitting with crossed legs and half-closed eyes. Experts believe this means they practised meditation.The oldest written evidence of meditation appears in the *Vedas* – a collection of poems and hymns from ancient India that were memorised and passed down by religious teachers for centuries before being written down around 1500 BCE. Historians have also found evidence of meditation in Egypt and China from around 6 BCE, and experts believe that people have been meditating since before recorded history.

Different types of meditation have been part of many religions, and throughout history, people have meditated to help them feel peaceful, to pray and to think deeply.

In the 21st century, meditation is a popular way to relax. There are meditation apps and classes online, so it's easy to learn how to meditate. People all over the world meditate, including those who are not part of a religion, in order to feel calmer and more creative.

3 Is meditation good for you?

Scientists have found that meditation is good for people in many ways.

Meditation:

reduces stress and **anxiety**

helps with control of **emotions**

helps with sleep

lengthens attention span

While research is still being done into how meditation helps us to be healthier, it's believed that meditation slows down our breathing and thoughts. When you take deep, slow breaths, your body relaxes because breathing slowly and deeply is a signal to your body that you are safe. The **vagus nerve**, which links the brain to the heart, lungs and digestive system, sends these signals of safety to the brain, and the brain tells the rest of your body that it can relax.

When you focus your attention on one thing, your mind can become clearer because it's no longer jumping from one thought to another. Meditation helps you grow aware of your thoughts, which can give you greater control over them. The more you think a particular thought, the stronger that thought's **neural pathway** becomes in your brain. So, when you are able to think calm, positive thoughts during meditation, those thoughts become easier and more natural for your brain to think, at any time of the day.

A relaxed body and a clear mind help us to make good choices, take care of ourselves and be kind to each other. The rest of this book guides you through a meditation.

4 Look

Take a moment to get comfortable and notice your breathing – take deep breaths in that fill your lungs, and slow breaths out, emptying your lungs.

Imagine sitting in a garden.

Look around: what can you see?

...

The leaves are so many shades of green.

You can see a tall apple tree full of fruit, a silver birch with its glowing bark.

Look again – in the flower beds, the leaves are not just green. You can see purple, red and yellow leaves. Leaves with frills and shiny round leaves like tiny pennies.

Look up – clouds pass across the sky. What shapes do they make?

Watch as they drift out of sight.

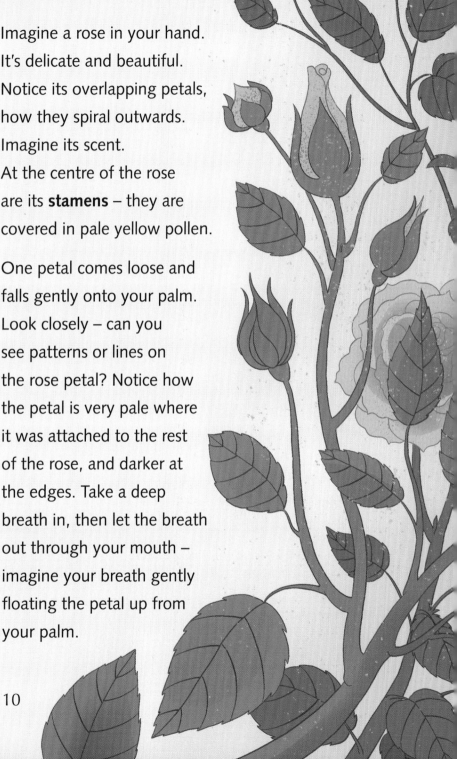

Imagine a rose in your hand.
It's delicate and beautiful.
Notice its overlapping petals,
how they spiral outwards.
Imagine its scent.
At the centre of the rose
are its **stamens** – they are
covered in pale yellow pollen.

One petal comes loose and
falls gently onto your palm.
Look closely – can you
see patterns or lines on
the rose petal? Notice how
the petal is very pale where
it was attached to the rest
of the rose, and darker at
the edges. Take a deep
breath in, then let the breath
out through your mouth –
imagine your breath gently
floating the petal up from
your palm.

There are so many flowers in this garden – too many to count. They grow in every colour of the rainbow – ruby red poppies, cheerful marigolds, a beaming sunflower, green **hellebore**, bobbing bluebells and delicate violets.

The bees are gathering pollen and **nectar** from the flowers to feed themselves and their families. Watch as a bumblebee travels from a rose, to a daisy, to a bush of bright fuchsias.

Imagine following a bumblebee's journey around the garden – think of the twists and turns, the things you'd see. Take a deep breath in, and breathe out with a soft hum, like the buzz of a bee.

5 Listen

What can you hear?

...

There are bees buzzing and birds singing.

You walk a little and find a small, round pool. Water is flowing from a stream into the pool. You can hear the water trickling over smooth rocks and into the pool. You pick up a tiny pebble and drop it gently into the water. Listen to it plop and watch the ripples travel across the surface of the water. Watch as the water returns to stillness.

Imagine being a fish in a calm pool. Take a deep breath in and as you breathe out, imagine blowing a clear, sparkling bubble.

You hear something else – a high, sweet sound in
the long grass nearby. It's a cricket, singing out of sight.
Imagine the cricket rubbing his wings together like a violin
to make a high-pitched sound.

A tiny bird flies by and swoops to take a sip of water from the pool. You can hear its little wings beating, the soft feathers carrying the bird up above the garden. It flies in a spiral up towards the sky, singing a joyful song.

Imagine you're the **conductor** of all the sounds in the garden – the breeze in the trees, the busy insects and the songs of many different birds. Take a deep breath in and out, listening to the rhythm of your breathing.

Now, imagine listening beyond the garden. What can
you hear?

...

A breeze travels over the tops of the trees, towards the sea.
You can hear the sea in the distance – the call of gulls high
above, and the soft crash of waves.

A boat bobs on the surface of the sea. It's filled with soft blankets and comfy cushions. Imagine the motion of the boat and the sound of the sea all around.

Picture that beautiful calm sea – watch a wave build as you breathe in, and as you breathe out let it break against the shore.

6 Taste

You've packed a picnic to eat in the garden – open it up and see what's inside. There's so much delicious food – fruits and vegetables, sandwiches and salads, cakes and pastries, and pink lemonade to drink.

You unpack little china plates, cotton napkins and glasses for the lemonade. Everything looks and smells good. You take a bite of all your favourite foods, one by one. Notice how they feel in your mouth, enjoy the different tastes.

Imagine the food in your tummy. Can you breathe in so deeply that your tummy **expands**? Now breathe out and notice how it becomes smaller.

21

Next, you pick up a plate of fruit. There are orange slices; they look like smiles. You squeeze a drop of tangy juice onto your tongue and it tastes sharp and sweet.

Run your finger along the dimpled skin of a slice and smell its fresh scent. Imagine the orange growing from a tiny white flower, changing from green to yellow to orange before it was ripe and ready to eat. Think about the sunshine, rainwater and all the energy from the orange tree that has gone into making this delicious fruit, just for you.

Breathe in and imagine a soft orange light travelling in with your breath, making your body feel full of energy. Breathe out, keeping the energised feeling inside.

You notice a butterfly land on a pink flower called a zinnia. It takes a drink of nectar. Its yellow wings open and close lazily as it drinks.

Can you imagine what it's like to be a butterfly?

Perhaps nectar tastes like honey mixed with lemonade, drunk through a straw. Imagine having wings even bigger than your body to carry you wherever you want to go, soaring over the garden and playing in the breeze.

Imagine your lungs are the wings of a butterfly.
As you breathe in, feel them expand and open.
As you breathe out, feel them close.

7 Touch

Put your hand on the grass. What does it feel like?

...

Notice the soft, tickly blades of grass and the cool earth beneath. Nearby is a tree called a horse chestnut tree with a thick, sturdy trunk. Reach your hand out to feel its rough bark.

Let your fingers wander over the ridges
and knots. Feel how different its texture is to
the texture of your hand. The bark is rough
against your skin, and scaly like a dragon.

Imagine the tree is a gentle, sleeping dragon.
Breathe with the dragon in through your
nose, and out through your mouth with
the sound of a soft, sleepy roar.

A leaf falls from the tree onto your hand. In spring, a horse chestnut tree's leaves are fine and soft. Come summer, they're thicker, and in the autumn, they turn orange, red and yellow.

This leaf is thick and bright green. Feel the leaf's veins and the smooth parts between them.

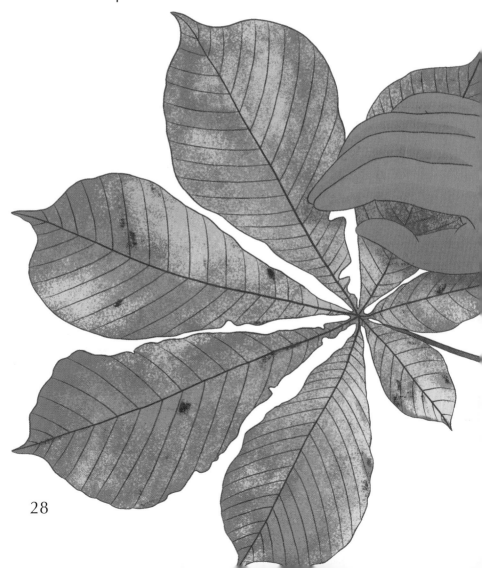

Trees breathe in carbon dioxide, and breathe out oxygen, keeping the air clean and healthy for us to breathe. Imagine the trees breathing with you.

The leaf looks like a giant hand. Walk your finger up and down the leaves – breathe in as your finger moves up, and breathe out as it moves down.

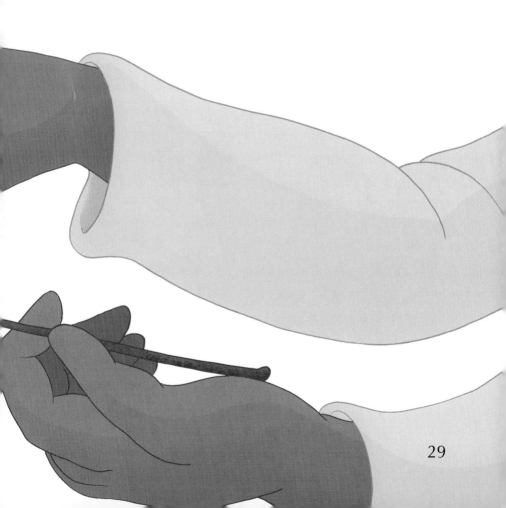

Imagine a horse chestnut landing softly on the ground next to you. Some people call these conkers – they have a spiky shell. The fall has split the horse chestnut's shell in two, and you can safely take it out without hurting your fingers.

You hold it in the palm of your hand. Its skin is so smooth and glossy, and it feels cool against your skin. This is the seed of the horse chestnut tree. Imagine it growing into a tall and mighty tree, with strong roots spreading into the earth.

Stretch your arms up to the sky, breathe in and imagine your branches growing tall. Breathe out and picture sturdy roots growing from your feet into the soil.

8 Smell

Breathe in – what can you smell?

...

Juicy grass, sweet roses, the orange from your picnic. Feel the air travelling in through your nostrils – notice how it's cool when you breathe in, and warmer when you breathe out.

Your breath is a natural rhythm that stays with you all day and all night. It brings oxygen into your body and takes carbon dioxide out. When we breathe deeply and slowly, our bodies understand that it's time to relax.

Breathe in the clean, fresh air of the garden and let it fill your body with a peaceful, calm feeling. Breathe out slowly and gently.

33

A warm breeze brings the smell of **lavender**, and other flowers and herbs to your nostrils. You step closer to the lavender bush, its pale green stems and tiny purple flowers sway in the breeze. You breathe in the scent of the flowers – it's delicate and herby, and it makes you feel a little sleepy.

You pick up a sprig of lavender from the grass and hold it close to your mouth. As you breathe in through your nose, imagine smelling the wonderful perfume of the lavender flower. As you breathe out through your mouth, imagine blowing the little flowers away.

A mouse peeps out of a hole in the ground. It looks at you with bright eyes and you decide to follow it. Imagine being a tiny mouse with a sensitive nose. The mouse uses its nose to guide you around the garden. The mouse can smell tiny crumbs of cake from your picnic, acorns from an oak tree, blackberries and wild strawberries hidden away in hedges.

As you breathe in, can you make your nostrils twitch like a mouse's nose? Now breathe out slowly and gently.

37

9 A feeling of calm

Has the garden brought you a feeling of calm?

Your mind is very powerful, and your imagination has the power to help you relax.

Think about the feelings in your body right now – are any of your muscles tense or uncomfortable? Think about each part of your body. Start at the top of your head and scan down over your face, your torso, your arms and legs, all the way to your toes.

As you breathe in, imagine you are breathing in the feeling of calm. As you breathe out, imagine you are breathing out any feelings of tension or anxiety.

Take this feeling of calm with you. Close your eyes and pay attention to how peacefulness feels in your body. Is there a particular part of your body where the peacefulness feels strongest? Perhaps it's your chest, your heart or your tummy.

40

Everybody feels emotions differently, and there's no right or wrong way to feel peaceful.

Focus your attention on the peaceful feeling. Each time you breathe in, imagine the peaceful feeling expanding. Each time you breathe out, you relax a little more.

You can imagine a garden like the one in this book whenever you want to feel calm. The words and pictures are ideas to get you started, and the garden in your imagination can be different in any way you choose. Think about the sights, sounds, tastes, smells and textures that make you feel calm and relaxed, and grow them in your imagination.

The more detail you put into your imaginary garden, the more powerful it will be for helping you feel relaxed. Your garden is there for you whenever you want to visit it – just close your eyes, take a deep breath and begin imagining.

Glossary

anxiety the feeling of worry, fear or nervousness

attention your mind's concentration

conductor a person who guides a group of musicians so their
    instruments sound good together

emotions feelings arising from thoughts and experiences

expands becomes larger

hellebore a poisonous but pretty flower

lavender plant used in perfumes and medicine for its
    calming scent

nectar sugary fluid made by flowers to attract insects

neural pathway series of connected neurons (brain cells) that
    sends signals from one part of the brain to another

stamens parts of a flower that produce pollen

vagus nerve a long fibre that carries messages between
    the brain and the heart, lungs and digestive system

visualisation using your imagination to create a picture in
    your mind

Index

How does your garden make you feel?

Ideas for reading

Written by Christine Whitney
Primary Literacy Consultant

Reading objectives:
- be introduced to non-fiction books that are structured in different ways
- listen to, discuss and express views about non-fiction
- retrieve and record information from non-fiction
- discuss and clarify the meanings of words

Spoken language objectives:
- participate in discussion
- speculate, hypothesise, imagine and explore ideas through talk
- ask relevant questions

Curriculum links: Science: Plants: identify and name common wild and garden plants

Word count: 2556

Interest words: meditation, emotions, anxiety, visualisation

Build a context for reading
- Ask children to share any times when they have visited a garden. What did they see there? What did they do there?
- Look closely at the front cover of the book. Ask children to discuss what they think the child is doing there and why.
- Read the blurb on the back cover. What things could be discovered in the garden?
- The book is an *information* book. Ask children to predict what information will be found in the book.

Understand and apply reading strategies
- Read together up to the end of p7. Ask each child to share three facts they have learnt about meditation. Encourage the use of the words *emotions* and *anxiety*, checking understanding.
- Continue to read to the end of p19. Ensure children's understanding of the word *visualisation*. Ask them to share how they felt whilst looking and listening in the garden.